Pebble® Plus

Australian Animals
Dingoes

by Lyn A. Sirota

Consulting Editor: Gail Saunders-Smith, PhD

Content Consultant: Dr. Mike Letnic
Research Fellow, School of Biological Sciences
University of Sydney, Australia

CAPSTONE PRESS
a capstone imprint

Pebble Plus is published by Capstone Press,
151 Good Counsel Drive, P.O. Box 669, Mankato, Minnesota 56002.
www.capstonepress.com

092009
005618CGS10

Books published by Capstone Press are manufactured with paper
containing at least 10 percent post-consumer waste.

Library of Congress Cataloging-in-Publication Data
Sirota, Lyn A., 1963–
    Dingoes / by Lyn A. Sirota.
    p. cm. — (Pebble plus. Australian animals)
    Includes bibliographical references and index.
    Summary: "Simple text and photographs present dingoes, their physical features, where they live, and what they
do"—Provided by publisher.
    ISBN 978-1-4296-4505-8 (library binding)
    1. Dingo — Juvenile literature. I. Title.
QL737.C22S59 2010
599.77'2 — dc22
                                                          2009040493

Editorial Credits
Gillia Olson, editor; Bobbie Nuytten, designer; Wanda Winch, media researcher; Eric Manske, production specialist

Photo Credits
Alamy/Bill Bachman, 19; Gerry Pearce, cover, 9, 15; Martin Harvey, 21; Terry Whittaker, 5
Ardea/Jean-Paul Ferrero, 13
Minden Pictures/Auscape/Jean-Paul Ferrero, 17
Peter Arnold/TUNS, 7
Shutterstock/Susan Flashman, 1, 11

Note to Parents and Teachers

The Australian Animals set supports national science standards related to life science. This
book describes and illustrates dingoes. The images support early readers in understanding
the text. The repetition of words and phrases helps early readers learn new words. This book
also introduces early readers to subject-specific vocabulary words, which are defined in the
Glossary section. Early readers may need assistance to read some words and to use the Table of
Contents, Glossary, Read More, Internet Sites, and Index sections of the book.

Table of Contents

Living in Australia

Dingoes are Australia's largest land predator. These wild dogs have lived in Australia for thousands of years.

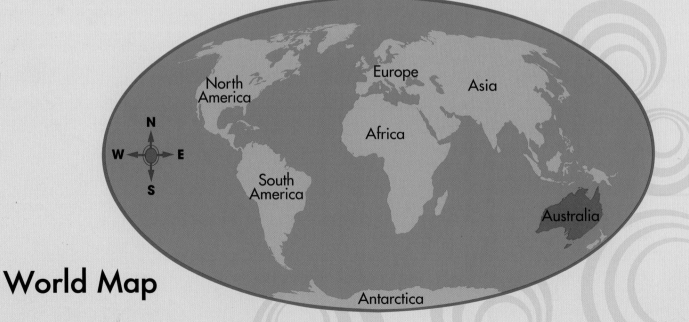

World Map

Dingoes live in Australia's
deserts, grasslands,
and woodlands.
They run in packs
of two to 12 dingoes.

Australia
Map

where dingoes live

Up Close!

Dingoes look like medium-size pet dogs. They weigh up to 49 pounds (22 kilograms). Dingoes have bigger jaws and teeth than pet dogs.

A dingo's fur is red-brown, black, tan, or white. Dingoes in hot places have short fur. In cooler places, their fur is thick.

A Dingo's Life

Female dingoes raise

their pups in dens.

Mothers usually have

four to six pups in a litter.

Sometimes litters are larger.

Instead of barking, dingoes
moan, snuff, and howl.
Sounds help pack members
find each other.

Hunting

Dingoes hunt kangaroos, rabbits, lizards, and anything else they can catch.

They sometimes prey on sheep or other farm animals.

Staying Safe

Ranchers kill dingoes that get too close to farm animals. Dingoes are safest when they live away from people.

Dingoes can mate with pet dogs.
True dingoes are becoming
less common.
Groups are working
to save true dingoes.

Glossary

den — a place where a wild animal lives

jaw — a part of the mouth used to grab, bite, and chew

litter — a group of young born to one mother at the same time

mate — to join together to produce young

moan — a long, low sound

pack — a group of the same kind of animals

predator — an animal that hunts other animals for food

prey — to hunt another animal for food

Read More

Gunzi, Christiane. *The Best Book of Wolves and Wild Dogs.* The Best Book of. New York: Kingfisher, 2003.

Koler-Matznick, Janice. *The Dingo.* The Library of Wolves and Wild Dogs. New York: PowerKids Press, 2003.

Internet Sites

FactHound offers a safe, fun way to find Internet sites related to this book. All of the sites on FactHound have been researched by our staff.

Here's all you do:

Visit *www.facthound.com*

FactHound will fetch the best sites for you!

Index

Word Count: 174

Grade: 1

Early-Intervention Level: 20